BENEATH THIS WEIGHT OF CHAIN

BRENDAN TRIPP

EPB-BT-022
an
ESCHATON BOOK
from

ESCHATON

P R O D U C T I O N S , I N C .

http://EschatonBooks.com

ISBN 978-1-57353-022-4

WHEN CLOSES OUT THE AGE

unwilling, almost,
we take the night
as if our own,
bolstered by decision
and stimulation in our mind
we brave the dark
in seeking out some strange decay
within the fabric of the world

> how little time remains
> before the crystal web is shattered
> and these cities fall to dust?

I chase a changing,
follow trails of transformation,
trials and tribulations
which are the tempered fire
within the epic of the soul,
these I seek before all else
to test the mettle of desire
against the grinding of that light

> when are these new dawns to appear?
> the starlight dwindles close to black
> without the promise of a sun

TOWARDS BRUTAL ENDINGS

layers float cross layers
images superimpose
standard time is deviated
we go adrift
lost amid some vortex flow
unanchored to a place
a time
unsure of heading
unable to define
the here or now
things become so sickening
when linearity is the mode
as lines run downward
from any point
all to worse bads
and greater ills
we see the planet dying
and see the race to blame
we are nauseated by these futures
and are angered by the past
no kind acts
will turn this tide
no good thrown to
this morass of evil
which change the course of doom
only now bold acts of cleansing
only now rash acts of fire
only now dire sweeps of killing
only now consuming pyres
there must be deeper darks
than the dull path of decay
there must be purging flames
to preserve the brighter sparks
within the closing of the curtain
and the dimming of the lights
when cold winds sweep unhindered
in the brutal dawnless night

THE ALTERNATIVE MADE INSANE

nerves hit panic's edge
        jangle
paranoias run too fast
        breed realities in their wake
fear and want and hurt and need
pump across unbalanced cores
        echoing madness
        following anguish with despite
                there becomes the terror
                knowing doom at every turn
                killing hope and prayer
        straws are clutched at
        longer bets are made
                to dodge the bullet
                escape the coming blast
there should be goodness in this night.
expectation should not be dread
                but, there it is
        vision sparks the ache inside
                burns like agony
        knowledge spurs the mind to flight
                with no place safe to hide
I can not rain or slow this time
                no reverse
                no control
foreshadowed is the sure defeat
                why must we act?
                why must charades be played
                hard into the teeth of pain?
        it is the essence of the world
        the pure defining of our state
like awaking
I lose these dreams,
like a blinding
by harsh and sudden light
there comes cold truth
        all these hopes are born to die,
        all these wants go unfulfilled:
                there is damning inherent to this life
so rise suicidal thoughts,
        the blade of leaving,
so comes the falling wish to die
                to make some meaning of the world
                a brutal, bloody sense
                which carves away
                these stupid empty lies

3

DREAMS NEVER QUITE ALIGNED

for this we have no fling
no analytic mode
     our categories fragment
     our naming wanders mute
our grasp extends,
at palpable figments waves.
after dreams attempts
to ground in concrete worlds
and generate the other side
       there is not
       enough of this
       there exists
       too much of theirs
       there are no
       clear marked escapes
         which lead beyond
         this blasted land
doorways seem to form amid the haze
but swirl back to the grey when our steps approach
    we should be watching
    tracing dreams
    counting reveries for these names
    fixing down the numbers
    to achieve an outlined book
       but there is distance and obscuring
       there are panes and panes of faulted glass
       which hold away our sight
again we set these lines to space
trusting in our sleeping creed
       but find they scatter
       do not align
       track curves against the grid of mind
where comes the dictate of the day.
the transcribing of the whole?
    we seek to read that tome,
    to order up the volumes past.
    and scan the scenes for patterns set
    by some cruel and hoary hand
       and hubris screams
       to change those lines
       to take the mantle of that pen
       retracing back the eons' path
       to write new starts to plots of man
so suspicion rises dark
that there is some recoil
and that the course of time
shall once again attack
and crush all hope once more

TRIADIC LEVELS FACING DAWN

1
where there arises wish and hope
there also lurks the fear of fantasy,
wherever there exists belief
the scent of blindness hangs heavily

       is there goodness?
       is there truth?
       are there worlds which are not pain?
       are there places which do no pulse
       with disappointments beat?
          I think not
          but wish it so,
          I know not
          but hope for it to be

2
there comes an image in the night
which echoes from some long ago
    it strikes me deeply
    somehow somewhere behind my mind
back beyond the self of now
there moves some vague remembrance
of places, names, and people
we knew or may have been

       how does one take the measure here?
       how can these stirrings be aligned
       so as to open doors on years
       so far into these pasts?

3
these wings prepare.
these shields and walls.
into battle we must lead
and know quite nothing of the field
       a darkness closes on the eye
       a bitter crawling grabs the gut

     a web is traced across that night
     which spreads arms open for our flight
     into absence, distance, fear,
     embracing conflict far and near

as this we take the chalice
and the challenge of that storm,
evolving through the whirlwind,
emerging from the vortex strong

NERVOUS SHIFTINGS WITHIN SLEEP

a nervousness hits
but the reality will not break
    all is held dream-like
    in a bubble of unwaking
I swim through thickness
in a world which is all sleep
where actuality fades from sight
and forms shift on the fly
        how to trust seeing
        when every eight changes?
        how to trust being
        when nothing is quite real?

new names enter
faces lurk behind a voice
unseen, unsorted,
ready to spring into view
        but not to knowing;
        we fear the very flash of it,
        the burning instant of stripped veils
    there seems some difference here
    but difference that yet rings the same
    to differences seen before
    in other visions, former states,
    past illusions gone to flame
        how can we take this trusting?
        how can we make this stay?

the layers of our sleep enfold
the waking state in waves of dark
all is muddled, all stands afar
all enters only as a shade
a shadow passing as by night
    a greater reach is needed
    a firmer grasp must take
    hold of these fleetings
        for in them lies the secret key
        the axe to shatter walls of dreams
        and free the obscured eye
who are these voices from without?
who stirs at the unconscious mind
and seeks to wake the crystal blade?
    I do not know them, nor can I see
    beyond this murky world of sleep

IN SUICIDE THE FINAL SAY

then these days explode
insanity takes its toll
and sweeps in wave-like from beyond
    to crush the senses
    bend the mind
    fold emotions into ache
and suddenly the planet shifts
and all is bars and walls and chain
and dungeons of unrighteous stone

        they strip that distance
        they strip away
        tearing, shredding
          like at skin
        to leave us bleeding
        to leave us bare
        and palpitating in the glare
          of suns of madness
          gleamed with poison light

what bondage holds us to this blade?
what blindness cloaks all real escape
    and leaves us groping through our pain?
    all this is folly
    all this is waste
    and tragedy not quite yet traced
we seek last answers
and find the hand of death
a soothing touch within our night

we knew no good
        could come of life
        no solace come from sweetness
          yet searched so hard
          to temper agonies of day
        in this we fail
        as all must fail
        who strive and yet would see
          how damning are these truths

THE PIT OF NO REDEMPTION

literally stopped
laterally stymied
    unable to progress
    unable to recede
here come days of ball and chain
here are the pressing times
        so arid now
        so blank and empty

the stones
they will not talk
the walls
they will not listen
    the vistas
    do not bloom
    with emotional translation
        all is hollow
        cold and hard
        belief has been discarded
        lost along the way
        all our days lie soaked in death
        and saddened with decay

there is a corner
we can not turn
there is a hill
we can not climb
there is a depth
we can not reach
there is a sky
we can not fly
    that voice is somehow locked away
    muffled, distant
    its content is a haze to us
    here in the sharp line cornered world

an echo comes
    a sight, a scent
recalling us to times before
        but there are shackles on our hands
        and these weights placed on our mind
we are contained here
immobile, stone
    there is no exit place within
    no safety valves without
we grasp no vision
nor hope for passage into light

TODAY, THIS WEEK, TOMORROWS, ALL

1
another dust settles
a different storm blows through the light
    still down to tiring
    still thirsting rest
a cyclone of our unbelieving eyes
builds preparation from all these far and near
        that some renewal
        be seen to come again
        and act as balms upon the rage
        fueled by more common flames

2
there's not enough
within the greater web
no slice so fine to be attached
to each and every need
    we churn the spaces
    mix the times
    and hope to froth sufficience
    out of the homogeneous sea
where comes insistence
that all our deeds be done?

3
layers and their strata
shift with friction undefined
    we can not know their goings
    we can not spell their lines
these elements too near to blend
within the planning of the day
    but not by our hand divided
    nor by our will delayed
how little off our way we turn
avoiding that tight wind

4
here tests the limits of our wait
when all our vectors make return
and prove the cosmos closed
        the sense becomes anticipation
        tied in with dreading
        and the shudders of the end
do these angles twist without
or erupt from within?
does the turning of the wheel
renew once more or flicker out to black?

THE WRONG PLACE IN THIS LIGHT

breakage comes in absence
schismed days
   not allowed
   not aligned
we move uneasy
we take the halting steps
into that void
not knowing pattern
or the reason of its place
      off into the emptiness
      which draws with gravity
too much swirling
the world is liquid
stiff and thick
with currents that move through and pull
along these vectors
through these eddies
which vortex down and spit us out
      onto those other planes
      without a rule
knowledge fragments brittlely
shard for shard like cutting ice
   all this is failing
   the cosmos drops
every plan has broke anew
and questions plague the mind
without a prayer of answer
without a dream of clearer sight
removed from places of wide view
     down in the stifling valley
     in lowness bought too cheap
thus comes the anguish
the pain which claws for freeing
against the walls of limit
and the stone embodied life
here now within
locked in this chest
   how might we leave
   without the blackest cloak?
I take these hands
and seek to pull
apart the joinings of the day
     but it is seamless
     whole yet empty in its void
we wait the final tracking
and the slow fade of release
   in what it is
   not what it does

BROKEN SEEDS OF SIGHT

1

we see no vision
we grasp no sights
there is flying
made as in dreams
over grey and unfeatured spheres
beneath a grey unyielding sky
all a line
all a vector cut through time
too vague on space
too emptied of the data flow
we sail unwilling
not quite approaching night

2

words are placed
yet not aligned
we find the letters formed of rage
and distance hiding in the mind
    dark the comers
    low the place of flight
    as tension coils
    and frustration rumbles far
        as though to shake the mountain
        and break the cliffs
        thrown down in anger
        violent to the sea

3

schism comes to lineage
rote is blasted out of time
and confusion reigns anew
    where goes this drifting
    towards what this dropping leads?
we craft returns
enter spaces long behind
in searching headings of this hour
fresh wrought from panic
and the speeding of the day
    if cycles are temporal
    is breath tomorrow's need?

THE DURATION OF THIS DARKNESS

we move through days
and watch dreams shatter
   there is no growing
   only change
   there's no achievement
   only marking
      items on a list of things
      that we have come to do
         and that unknowing of the plan
         so that we act in blindness
         stumbling on from deed to deed
         while groping for the pattern

it seems no good
all joys are hollow
based upon a flawed first ground
which won't allow succeeding
   as every good is not the best
   and every win is not the all
      and every pleasure
      does not free us from this life

an emptiness pervades this being
a void that harbors not intent
   almost as though
   some key were missing
   almost as though
   we lacked some sense
      denied the knowledge of our sight
      or deaf and not suspecting sound
         unable to frame the question
         or plead for absent information
         of which we only just suspect
         by the shallowness we feel

there is a drive within this breast
which cedes no ground to words
yet grasps at every hidden thing
as to squeeze it for its juice
   when opens up that sapient font
   or those tomes clear to read?
      this is a mystery to these eyes
      which fully beg to see

ARISING, TURNED TOWARD LIGHT

await the vision
yet put off
strung along those days
which are not tolled
with remembrance's bells
as these are

we move to heights
and pray for clarity
that seeing
will lift the common breast
and charge the soul with light
amid sweet darkness

so much fills up
this living's days
as though we need more life
than one to feed our time
there is a grinding in this press
but one that brings a brighter shine

a wavy thread
links dark and lightness
which builds on dreams
the vaster hopes for which we pray
for we've glimpsed that Eden
and now ache to walk its way

these cycles still are turning
amid new cycles and counter others
we feel them trace
out these patterns which define
our world, our being, our souls and self
like lanterns quickly in the night

how dearly there desires perfection
within the very core of life
all else pales
and washes ashy grey from out our sight
as towards those beaming, glorious hues
we stumble, stagger, and still quest

A CYCLE RARE TO SEE

we approach corrosion
frantically trying to return
to points of plans
locations of intent

these hours bleed
with new efficiency
and run a total
which is hidden In the wings

blocks of concept
are rearranged in minds
which disallow deletion
but press on without sleep

temptation holds reaction
against the plotted day
we are uneasy
at losing coming gleam

layers of recall contract
and jostle for these thoughts
as though those yesterdays became
in these spheres tomorrow's dream

we search for months
to hold our meanings
we sort through years
discarding what we've been

how view has changed
when seen from ceilings
hovering observant
at what has become two

by numbers planes begin to crack
there are divinings held in this
we can not read but on their surface
which shines too pointed light

beings enter from the dark
but not from darkness come
I swing my arm to cast them off
yet they lurk beyond the shell

taste the power
beyond the curve of day
it pulls me searching
moth-like to its flame

PARTITIONS THROUGH UNSTEADY NIGHT

1
voices maintain
without clear instruction.
as yet without text;
we feel this coming
but know not how to be prepared
and wonder blankly
if dreams fit into hopes
and hopes cause answered prayers

2
stared at these words
that once we knew
the concepts still align with soul
but labels blur
without a handle to attain
a grasp thereof
to form again the will to speak
in eastern shaded tones

3
there are the halls
of stores downtown
there are the rooms
of hotels on the coast
there are the yards
of long agos
when memory presents
what details must we know?

4
blurred focus
colors not of sight
yet comes a visit
wracked with lines
which holds to value
these few scenes
here arrayed
in their many forms

5
I must search out the details
and force them on the mind
fuller scope must be attained
that every aspect fit
the hidden form must take new shape
that its channels be the true
and stand ready for the power
when that hour tolls at last

BAD TIMES NEW DAWNING

the torture time invades
makes all things edgy
bent in spasmed forms

there is a precipice within
and we madly dance along its edge
screaming angry at its void

the killing urge Is near to this
we look for danger
and try to corner blood

we feel the fibers bursting
under tension, in this stress
and know not when the blade will fall

no violence is enough
each smash results in smaller stones
which must be pulverized anew

there is a drive behind
the uneasy clawing gut
which never knows of rest, release

our frustration blasts through time
and is met with insufficience
at every turn and sight

hands do not destroy enough
we dream of monsters
huge machines preset to kill

how putrescent seems the race
fools preying on the fools
like rats that eat their own

no functions last
all systems fall to decay
as vision fades

it all is history
in madness, blindness, stupid life
repeated on and on again

PERFORMANCE GRID

turn the hand
present the palm
extend the arm
flex from elbow full in front
twist and raise across a curve
past the brow and into space
sweep across and back to rest
shift the other
with the flow
in parallel return to front
swing to the heart
and back down joined
pressed at the tips
as if in prayer
with one step back
they split and slide
descending now to flank the sides
tracing angles of the slope
of temples long before forgot
close the eyes
and balance weight
await the coming of the voice
to speak before encroaching light
the heat and murmur
hang far off
in distances defined by lines
which we are not to cross
     break then
     relax
     from tensions ease
     all joints shift planless
     and connections break
      feel the charge then
      in the air
      expectant tracings
      from the one crowd mind
then comes the time of words
they eat upon your hand
unknowing what is what
as if broken to the dark
weave within that grey-scale
walk the hazy line
your voice can carry crushing weight
as though talking for the muse
from out your silence
embodied in the simple form

17

QUADRANTS OF UNEASY LIFE

1
night splits open
to its seed
desperate kernel
precious like jewel
    harbor this fragment
    which is all we're allowed
    suck up its nectars
    like the rain

2
material fades
slips from grasp
layers of need
fight with desire
    these are plans
    yet to form
    intentions unburdened
    by embodying light

3
where is the spike
which pierces skulls?
we feel its pain
but not its sight
    from eye to crown
    stabs the blade
    there is not sleep in this
    nor movement made

4
days are counted
set in line
a bitterness wells up
to taint the time
    never has a joy
    graced these dates
    always sadness bears
    the mantle of our being

OF WILL TO BREAK AWAY

you wait for years
amassing textures
piling block on block
day on day
without a meaning
without clear goal
it is a rocket sled without a track
an uncontrolled parade of time
which locks to forward and will not steer
will not take the subtle guide

    there is a voice that screams within
    yet so far off as to be faint
    it begs for disengaging life
    to find some quiet
    and carve some calm
    out of the chaos of this world
    that every word of truth be heard
    and open lightness
    brighter than the sun
    within the spirit and the soul

how to deal
with chain and eye?
how to bargain
with the pressure sales of death?
    there is a world we know beyond
    there is a place that holds the good
    there is a peace the mind can touch
    off behind the stone walls of this cage

how to tear away the veil
and stare in vision
clean, crisp, cold and true?
how to pulverize the blocks
and open being
into wide, expansive life?
    it is the moment
    of cutting lines
    it is the juncture
    of hidden routes
    it is the turning
    of willingness surprised

SINCE THE LAST GAME AT EBBETS

these strange anniversaries
hang in parallel
unsuspected through the years
perhaps not even cared if noted
or pointed out before
but in this passing
the date rings off the page
and makes one wonder
of rightness of a name
or if those before had passions
which would lead to such surmise
to mark the shifting
from one long ere
into new life
led blankly in a bliss
which did not bear the weight
of that commemoration
to juxtapose
like patterns placed
end to end
and span to span
stretching through the decades
awaiting like an untouched tomb
to be uncovered
to be exposed
to touch the hazy light of day
and cause a wonder
not based on life
but run along repeating grids
as though each history returned
and made again its presence
in the subtle call
the formation of the play

IN GRIP OF FRANTIC HANDS

bad confluence
of streams of rage
every soul is edgy
every mind insane
I am not apart
from madness here
I tumble in the rapids' flow
which churns with panic
and foams over into hate
flashing violent
erupting into flame
    bad place
    inauspicious juncture
    why can't we flee
    why can no escape be found
    to grasp safe haven
    and duck the searing tide?
these swirls now spiral through the mass
spinning off our senses
dizzying our minds
we find no focus in the storm
nor can we grid to hold a point
and make it guidance for our time
to pull us on
and gird our will
within the chaos of this life
    under evil's sway
    we sink beneath the waves
    all is shadowed
    paralleled by mythic force
    which speaks no doctrines
    by which we could be saved
all these lines
are scattered, spilled
without the whim of order
denied a pattern to define
they fall upon the seasoned earth
and scream for taking
in their crossings plead
for elevation
for conception to array
some reason placed upon their forms
which would be telling
and set to be
beyond their shattered sight

PULLED AWAY TO DREAM

to islands
you see the call
the music wafts on many airs
and rings within the head

nearing
we can almost feel the breeze
the sun
and hear the churning
of such warm seas
beyond the rise
just there

images all appear
shift and meld
counter and blend
we are the places we have been
and ache for being
these fantasies we have not seen

I soar as eagle
take the vista on strong wing
my home is of the mountain
and savage on the plain

strange tides
bear us all away
I speak these currents
in folded corners of my soul
where wounds reside that never heal
and plead for journeys never made
off into more sharp-lit lands
which hold the essence of the dream
just beyond our waiting lips

know the pulsing of the stone
lash with storms upon the shore
find extent beyond the self
that from its chains be freed
to be amongst these
to walk these ways
and feel the reaching of the real

THESE VISITS SQUARED WITH MIND

these prophesies
ring back through years
and layer with
the jested curse

we lose our place
can not connect
drift unsteering
between these worlds

now turn on flow
and fight with fate
there is no cause
no trail behind

familiar sights
fill inner eyes
without intent
or meaning seen

wings restless grow
locked down to earth
denying flight
within this time

too many names
align with need
delay the course
of too few days

we must return
renew our link
to places gone
lost down the years

a winter scene
revisits cold
unfelt, unknown
as stranger here

rebellion forms
within the heart
unwilling to
cede all the reins

we can not let
this darkness fall
another road
leads us away

STRAPPED ONTO WHEELS OF LIFE

darkness into blackness
delving into depth
everything becomes unwell
all is tainted
bearing stains of poisoned hope
wishes that have fallen dead
corrupted by the stuff of day
twisted tight against the mind
    we are murdered
    taken down
      and out
      and shot
    disassembled
    broke from wholeness into parts
    which warp and battle
      forging war
      one with the other
      the mad melee
    a churning chaos filled with rage
    which destroys the very self
        but not enough
        not far enough
        it will not take
        the killing self away
all these things leave little room
no exit clear through which to flee
we are frenzied
and grow violent in the trap
striking out to just strike out
smashing with our vengeance hands
that would destroy
that would crush the very world
    and yet our waiting bears some fruit
      rotten fruit
      too long away
    there Is no joy there
    we know no joy
    living drags on in despair
      that nothing forms as we intend
      and nothing grows as we would wish
    every act is just more weight
    amassed to grindstones on our necks
      we seek the water that would free
      us by its drowning
    every day another tick
    off of some schedule
    some sentence made
    to break us on this wheel

FROM PARADIGMS OF STEEL

all these years
all these years
shuddered by number
maddened by rage
broken down empty
    almost beyond
    the point of care
    almost beneath
    the bile of self contempt
    framed hard by living
    held to the killing glare

there is no focus
no current for the sweep
we founder aimless
within too-structured days
unable to create within
what is missing from without
    we hear the echoes
    of meaning gone before
    but heed this little
    so burdened by our time
    tied up in many webs

yet wanderings ensue
off into aways
but never far
and never home
forgotten as a pledge
    there is no fitting
    there is no match
    just void and black
    failing, falling
    dropping down to lower states
    unable to redeem

ours no future
ours no hope
all becomes a trap in life
and bears shackles
greater with each dawn
and its weight of chain
    only breakage
    seems to free
    casting off the cloak of day
    to slip from context
    clear into escape

DIRECTIONS FROM SOME QUEST

art thou off planet?
    it seems bizarre
    not possible
    not capable
    these do not exist
    far off
    in the blackness
    in the vastness
    amid the emptiness of space
      and yet they speak
      coursing through the veins
      and singing on the wires
      not quite heard
      but sensed behind the ear
      from the silence split

art thou enfolded in the night?
    we walk on city streets
    and search the jaguar
    we seek the jungle
    but find only the brick
    and phantom cars
    there is not enough
    to build a practice here
    too little sand to grasp
      talk beneath the grid
      scream between the planes
      this holds running in its soul
      not free and joyful
      fleeing to escape
      what lines and angles mean

art thou within me?
    surely there are tides
    pulling from beyond
    I am all distant
    massive as the sea
    something guides this movement
    something leads it on
    drifting ever towards an end
    horizons fail to scan
      a pulse brings up a reason
      and echoes that below
      we feel connection
      and touch the fibers of the link
      down to the center
      weaving up the whole

CONDEMNED TO HORRID TIMES

down
life cycles down
plummets down
all is falling
is failing
is crippled
all is poison
and leads to death

existence is corruption
is decay
good's a shadow
which passes and is gone
a phantom
lacking substance
a dream
a wish beyond a prayer

all lines
all angles point as knives
each aligns
skewers mind
at the center
the target zone
butchered by a world
always set to kill

evil
is the fabric of the race
is the stuff of being
is the tide of life
nothing grows
nothing thrives
all is destruction
vile, putrescent rot

no escape
no fleeing from the chain
we wait to die
and yet must live
we ache to leave
and yet are caged
entombed here
a hell denied our night

FOR BREAKING FROM THESE DEPTHS

about these failings
who can say,
what comments form
which grasp the span
or plumb the depths
of our abyss here?
>we feel so fractured
>so damaged
>so deeply in defeat
>that no light goodness can repeal
>the sentence of our anguish
>so heavy on these heads

it is not enough to be away
to reach for distant glimmers
and even briefly taste
their scintillations
this will not drag us from this hole
and lead us to completion
>all striving comes to naught
>each path finds blankness
>each hallway ends in walls
>and we return here
>empty and too aged
>to ever hope for better chance

these hours bleed away
we feel them go
like lifeblood draining from a wound
that never hopes to heal
gored by life and prayer and sight
we are left here to decay
>yet in the nighttime
>come fresh dreams
>not those of sleeping
>but those of will
>which show a stripping off the world
>and building it anew

from this charnel house of pain
sounds a rumbling
like geysers seeking out the sky
to rend the rocks and stone of penting
and blast away what holds all back
in darkness and confusion
>it is the moment of the grave
>held low now
>but dawn comes horrid to their eyes
>new crafted by all change
>far too brilliant
>for them to stand the sight

THE PATH WHICH CALLS TO HEED

channels running below the ground
I hear thunder in the hills
there is lightning amid the soul
and a fire beneath the breast
     into connection advance
     stripping off the shell of man
     cloaking with clouds, with rain
     grasping the current of life

I am one with heat
all elements are in me now
we reach behind the veil
and grasp the power

     deep within,
     these temple stairs
     leading up
     we layer times
     become one with the now
     woven into trails of then
     force fresh ritual
     enact new seeds of light
     and take the chalice
     which presents from out these depths
     and drain it to the stone
     completing cycles

I survey the jungle's eyes
reaching out across the miles
there is nothing we can't see
emboldened by the draught of sight

pulse of darkness
violence of the storm
it is in your hatching
that I come to life
     known in being
     alloyed from nature's gait
     our path is wrought here
     glistening with stars' delight

LONG INTO THE TRAP

1
we can not make
the transition
this expanse
is far beyond our grasp
    bodhichitta
    we can not attain
    liberation
    dances from our hand

2
mind settles into shallows
runs within the rut
    we ache for tremors
    to blast beyond this
    we claw at stone
    to find the freeing flash
we hear the echoes of old distance
in which we know that light yet lies
        but we are stymied
        blocked amid our quest
        held by the folding
        of this gutter's walls

3
all of these fears now focus
hard on this one quick scene
converting it to symbol
of fleeing and the chain
    the seeing eye goes blank
    as history retains
      all secrets
      all future acts
    we can not form the knowledge
    to be sure within our step

4
frustration stabs
like broken glass in shoes
plunging, shocking
gouging with each stride
    we hear the murmur
    of other pasts
    we sense a pattern
    which we can not restrain
there is no fabric
which we can rend
there is no substance
to meet the fury of these hands
    can vision be attained
    once it has died?
    can voices be rekindled
    once their ash has spread?

5
we seek to read these tomes
    we seek to take their magic
we seek to know this lore
    we seek to grasp the wisdom
we seek to hold those reins
    we seek to wield that power
6
the mornings are corrupted
    days of promise
    are dragged through slime
the hours stretch blankly
    nothing is made here
    nothing but shame
weeks tick away unmourned
    each fades too slowly
    we ache for death
the hollowness perverts us
    all is bitter
    with cynical bile
eyes seek to fade from seeing
    too painful vision
    amid dark cells
suffocation haunts us
    we can not live
    yet will not die
7
it seems no good
I am adrift, in limbo
caught between aspiration
desperation and despair
    the hand would take
    any weapon's blade
    to cut me free
it seems too late to grow
and too far to retreat
I can not act to rise
and can not move to flee
    no path allows
    the swift decay
    or sweet awakening

THE SIREN OF THE QUIET EYE

what are the aspects of the deed?
it shimmers faintly
dull amid the glowing fires
and offers no resistance
when these vectors come to play
  in those days
  are retribution
  in those places
  a vale of tears
  in those times
  come revolutions
   and the subtle shifting
   of some dark wind
it is of the wider mass
brought down by volume
deflated by these numbers here
 we can not count this
 we can barely know the name
 and form retention
 of disassociated face
 not focused in recall
but you know
you harbor this
you touch the outlines
and the edge
you store its data in your files
and spew it out at questions' light
   it is not enough to be the need
   but comfort forms in that decay
I turn towards leaving
and make to go
while sensing dawns beyond the day
things breaking wider
In wilder style
offering up a total change
a shift beyond all these intents
  and silence calls
  upon these tapes
  without a tracing for the mind
   no hooks
   no leads
   no logic zone
  it is the opening of life
  not seen enough by common eyes
  but heard in distance
  a sweetly song far off

REFLECTIONS IN THAT FLOW

nothing quite like
moon shining on water
In pavement puddles
glinting off mica
in cement surface
late at night
in the city's quiet
only rustled
by the passing of these trucks
heading somewhere
with intent

       we await for the unfolding
       like in the mountains' mist
       which breaks in sunlight
       and opens up the view
       gripping at the heart
       rocketing the spirit up
       and out into expansive ways
       which are close to nature
       yet hidden in most days

others skim the surface
and do not dive
we ache to plummet
into those shiny depths
and see the colors
and myriad forms
to take away the wonder there
and bring it to the world
but they know nothing
of that realm
how we wish they even cared

       these sleep but fail to dream
       or dream yet fail to wake
       ruts are cut amid the lines
       marking goings
       time and time again behaved
       like simple robots
       beings with one program set
       that do no growing
       but only break

BROKEN TIMES, LOCKED INTO RAILS

without infusion
the greed just swells
and makes nothing possible
only detritus
only leftovers of times before
stacked all around us
built up as by life
into the kingdoms of no meaning

we spin our plans
and in their webs catch failure
disappointment feeds us
makes us frail and damaged
unable to progress
unwilling to forge efforts
to climb to better heights
that are to us the same

we pull in the empty net
filled only with these lists
we search for fullness in the wash
but find structures of foam
that blow away in coming winds
and empty purpose
just as hollow as the dream
which makes this all seem real

these patterns move us
we fracture will
and paralyze all our intent
there is no going
all things are lines
and we are carried by their ways
into motions long pre-set
awaiting our arrival

that world is tainted to its core
its absence is its only base
and yet it grabs us
drags us screaming into shapes
which do not show our form
what night releases, what day brings clearing dawn
to change the orbit of this place
and free us from its jaws?

HEAVY WITH THE WEIGHT OF CHAIN

all the aches intrude
we can not see the day
madness is around us
and nothing lets in good

    I want to know that light
    I want to see those lines
    I want to grasp the patterns
    deep within the subtle flow of life
    but can not here
    locked up inside
    I have no access to the world
    chained into artificial places
    which are not me
    which are not mine
    which seem to want to crush the life
    out of the realer self

most others seem the same
locked in their own small hells
what horrid world is this we make
that denies us all our lives?
what insanity has gripped the race
that divides us from the earth?

    it seems so evil
    and those who fall for it
    blindly, willingly,
    enthusiastically, wholeheartedly,
    they seem the demons of this pit
    for they would stamp out every spark
    of light we may let gleam

this sickens, this kills
a poison washes over us
and cuts us to the quick

    dark place
    sad world
    I have almost ceded to your bonds
    all hopes of living free
    there is no guiding
    we see no paths
    nothing opens up a way
    that we might be away
    and be in joy

PLACE OF BEING, BIAS SIDE

formations of inversion
taken to extremes
    not with shitting motion
    not denied the blade
there is dark current to this day
pulling our poor hearts apart
    with no concern
    no consideration
It is the weight of planets dragging down
the tidal wrench of planes in passage
manifesting meshing with
    a form of feeling
    a mode of pain
    a sinking drawing into depths
        which have not seen before
we take the sizes of the year
and make of them a better web
excusing self away from tracks
worn deeply in the old
    it is not known
    within the standard time
    it is not traced
    amid the common space
        it is beyond
        and yet effects us here
        running down
        like clocks and rivers flowed
no matter what becomes of being
there echoes something of that past
    written nowhere
    barely sensed
    alternated with our eyes
abstraction comes abrupt
and we decay to symbol
moving vectors
lines and planes
    spiraling through motives
    involving into change
still we know the distant roles
and dance the movements of their state
    unsuspecting how or why
    yet in precision's sway
there comes the nighttime with an ache
which beckons us to some inside
drawn upon some mental slate
whose directions are without control

NOT DELIVERED FLIGHT

not enough to be believed
not enough to care
    land is glowing
    land afire
    skies are lit with burning red
    night crackles with the flame
    all consuming
    all destroyed

sickness bleeds into the heart
every angle seems to kill
every facet blunt, traumatic
swinging pressure to the face
    no goodness here
    no ease
    everything now cycles tense
    twisting up perception's lines

    another time must be the way
    a different place must fill intent
    alternating views of self
    must be the only cause to be
        for in this vileness
        an error seems
        and from this horror
        a waking would seem right
    ours the emptiness inside
    mocked by echoes from far planes
    where proper paths had formed of choice
    and power surged and blessings rained

how to fly,
how to be away?
    chains that are not chains
    yet lock us to this ground
    walls that are not walls
    still keep us sealed in dark
        we derive from nothingness
        the essence of our being
        we distill from anguish
        the liquor of our dreams
      it is a naked place within
      that bleeds profusely from the blade

known from knowing
seen from sight
    it is the blackness delved
    not ever finding light

STARS FROM DARK ASIDES

1
it becomes unwell
it degrades
it allows no leeway
it forbids no rage
it enters sideways
it enfolds what's vile

2
disjointed patterns bump
in sudden stop
and twisting steel
the days are not as planned
not arrayed by means of thought
nor intentional

3
too long go journeys
no count erodes
no amassing takes
every step seems far behind
the furtive goal upon horizons
not held or ever reached

4
darkness hovers
morbid clouds swoop in
all light is arcing sparks
nothing like real day
focused sadly
in times before the storm

5
never is belief entailed
we slash slow distance
never are these freedoms glimpsed
we term the stone rank
never do our visions stream
we only see desiring

6
take apart these dreams
piece by piece unlabeled
strew them across the fields
and pray for crystal flows
like rains of ice
and mercury descending

HERE SHATTERED WITHOUT DREAMS

there portends the seizure
all becomes corrupted
it is of derision
hard and broken
placed within the night

is there nothing left
which sparks the self?
there is drowning here
waves wash with depth
blur to indistinction

the freedom split
seems never to be found
our hours are denied us
twisted In black day
never to release

demand enfolds demand
no degrees are open
no desires met
for this is prison
bars of our own design

others form arisings
transgressing bounds of dreams
gird by echoes
these intents would melt
into absence's blade

no vectors proceed
the web decays
life maintains its pattern
far beyond the core
left abandoned here

pain manifests all sides
redoubling, reflecting
in disappointment and dismay
there darkness takes our hand
and leads us to its keep

WASTED PLACE OF RUINED TIME

wracked again
not finding exit
a way to leave
to be away
    life is shit
    sometimes
    when all the goods can't tip the scales
    against that horrid, crushing weight
    which presses on each day
    and thrusts desperation into night
        you know its name
        you feel its chain
        it is the drowning amid the blind
        the smothering of all our sight

we see the glimmers of release
as though small creatures
through veils of heavy leafs
the images of what might be
dart through obscuring
and dash away when we would grasp
their fleeting forms
        this itself is saddening
        and adds mass to the whole
        we ache so much for that escape
        and all the crystal shining joys
        upon that other side
        that their sheer distance is a pain
        which we might not endure

here is our cycle
the rut of our return
we can not lift the yoke
which binds us to our doom
        nothing is freeing
        there comes no portal
        no way for us to flee
in all these hours flushed away
is there anything which builds of time
something solid and unyielding
before the senseless march of years?
        nothing grows herein
        this is the wasteland
        the empty chalice of our tears

FROM DARKNESS FAR AWAY

practiced on the edges
the hazy zones where none can know
and be one with the tide
    these arrive
    made sharp in honing
    upon the ancient stone
    acute in their desiring
    their mission and their blade
we then snap back
wishing to awake the self
and be assured
    that this is but a dream
    a fantasy built of the miles
    and decades we have spent
    in ceaseless going
    in unrelenting spite
        but, no,
        and stranger yet
        this rises to the top
        and bobs upon the surface
        giving glisten 'neath the moon
        and horror in reflection's light
        when knowing is
        and being does
nothing then remains herein
all is scattered
and wiped clean from the slate
we fall useless
used and cast aside
    there becomes a pulse within
    echoing uncertain drums
    sensed in the dark outside
something makes its meal
something causes entitles
spun out from those depths
to feed upon the stuff of souls
and tear into these nights
        amid that vision lurks one truth
        which grips with terror at the gut
        and shatters seeing's base
to know it there
evade it here
to trace its pathways
without the tearing steel
that is the motive
that is the way
to open up the chasm deeps
with violating light

41

TO NEVER GO TO SEA AGAIN

downside formed of loss
the sudden mass fell from the sky
    unsuspected
    unprepared
what was the triad's point
is now lopped off
what was the constant shell
is now shattered from the soul
    left naked
    without defense
    scared and gaugeless
    so exposed
these ache without bleeding
yet scar us deep within
the tides of our attachments
are torn into the storm
and churned in fits of anguish
    of what once was
    but now is gone
    of what we were
    but now are not
    and what again is never seen
we cry for this
and weep for bitter years
now tossed away
run into shades of myth
        no brightened coat
        will hide the pain preserved
        within that sanctuary
        new buried with its gods
it is a history betrayed
a long time ally cruelly slain
    and on these hands
    the scent of blood

            count the number
            then align
            these tell their stories
            nevermore
            across the traces we have known
            the memory will only fade
            into that distance
            without a reach
            deep in darkness
            we can not journey through

SEARCHING FOR THOSE WAYS

is it there
within the fiber,
the stuff of life,
the weave which moves with day?

is it open
and able to be found,
or does it hide with cruel intent
and seek to see us screaming
at its absence from this place?

is it real
and structured In our world,
or does it lie like shadows
cast by some other sphere
to briefly touch our field?

is it there,
can we reach it,
can we make of it
a jewel adornment now?

    nothing is clear within this life
    still we see the swirlings
    and track the patterns behind the light
    which give to us perceptions
    of what lies hidden
    and what lurks waiting behind the day

    we try to bridge that gap
    and grasp across the boundary
    the shining ring
    the halo bright
    to make a total change within
    the mundane borders of this World

        go beyond these walls
        and so slough off these chains
        soar to undreamed heights
        beyond these vile remains

        take the fire of stars
        to re-spark inner light
        invert forms of dark
        resanctifying night

NO DOORWAY TO THE GARDEN

there is no forming
of sense from this
the core is damaged
broken down by too much night
torn apart by counter tides
and gored by visions
of talons on the wing

we drift down into fear
nagging doubts of what is safe
and what is poison
swirl within the dizzied mind
making all abusive grey
a moiré of hard reds and greens

we can't detach from fiction
and are myth within the world
knowing no decision
we stumble with the blind
reeling from the wounds of life
unable to find focused form
or vector from one site

no joy is ceded
in distance or return
we ache departure
from the mundane to the real
but veils prevent us
binding us to common chain

when will the riving split
asunder the projection?
what blade or force cut time
and leave a doorway through?
I am damaged by this place
and need to find a side
which holds belonging's key

known but now forgotten
held but now released
what remnant trace within
repeats as by an echo
and speaks the truer name
that these might then be one?

FROM MOVEMENT YET UNGROUNDED

1
entering the palace
striding down the marble halls
glancing at the niche-held dead
while passing towards the center court
    not arriving
    falling through
    exiting in dissolve fades
    on to other lands

  there Is a crispness
  edging to this air
  the sun burns distant
  just at the horizon
  small creatures stir and call their names
  moistness hangs upon the rocks
    which swirl and open
    pulling in

    metal clangs on metal
    thunder issues from the hooves
    of charging beasts of war
    blood soaks the soil we crouch upon
    as we close our eyes and wait
      slipping inward
      falling down the thick descent
      which leads to other planes

    2
    darkness holds there
    within the mind
    opening few lights to see
    the mode of our confinement
    where we have journeyed
    where we have strayed
    lost from vectors of the day
    distracted into deeper paths
    and curled beneath crude sight
    which is true blackness
    knowing colors of the dark
    we find there answers
    and read there tomes
    which can not bear recall
    upon the surface
    in flotsam life

PLACES OF THE NEED TO FREE

1
down to abstraction
where nothing works
we are the alien
yet apart
wishing just to step aside
out of this world
out of this storm
into clearer, vaguer realms
where intuition calls the shots
and not obsession
not emotion
not fixation's frantic drives
which churn this race
into a frenzied mass

2
all the levers look the same
but some bring chaos
some bring fire
we jab out blindly at controls
for which there is no training
and hope to find the one that frees
unsealing doors
releasing to escape
from this chamber
out of this cell
to walk in brighter filtered light
where waits the garden
calling now
in coolness and relief

3
influences flow from words
as by incantations made
over ancient tomes
we see these weave a tapestry
in colors unsuspected
run with power
twined in unlike forms
yet intimating perfect wholes
which we can not perceive
we take these threads
and follow
we trace their lines
and seek to know
the distance where they lead

PLACED AWAY, INSISTENCE

everything becomes devoid
vistas bleeding
worlds on drain
an ashen, hollow place results
like ancient sitcoms
when we have lost the jokes

frantic reaching for the dream
devolves to grasping
clutching tight the mine, mine, mine
losing balance in the swing
between the nothing and the all

I can not be one in this
I splinter, fragment
a mirror dropped on its edge
splitting into many
with tiny shards
which never will make whole

we are blind here
we can not see the light beyond
blocked by mountains
higher than the sky

something chimes in distance
but these can not be synched
with doctrine's tracings
forays run out to attain
the baubles of that time
but disjoint cycles rise
and clash against our pure intent

the weight of graves o'ershadows
the message of the sun
we lowly whistle dirges
and know the time has come
for crushing out all joy

strong cravings point the arrow
into the outward flight
assuming all futility
but driven yet to leave
into those outsides
and every facet of the gone

ANTICIPATION OF THESE BLASTS

bastardized arrangements
connections in the storm
like lightning searing through the sheets
of blinding torrents
violence ripping out the structure
of every mode extant

> we ride this blindly
> entwined yet not involved
> our form is pierced by acid blasts
> which pass unmarking
> except by leaving poison dregs
> which embitter and confuse

we would take the name and crush it
we would stand apart from worlds
and by our will recant
all allegiance to that side
which drives all crazy
and fosters nothing sane

> here is the moiré whirl
> a matrix which holds wild insides
> and fibers which would undo space
> without a caring
> beyond the point of hate
> splintered into million barbs

the press moves on relentless
there is no real release
or relief from common states
nightmares curl within the brain
and bring a taste of twisted day
to sweet enfolding sleep

> from downward motions up
> the numbers won't attest
> or make that entrance gape
> enough of that, enough
> there are too many things within
> to open up a gap in doom

RECURRENCE WHEN TRANSFORMED

everything becomes
encircled
systems decline and fail
running downward
always in return
our eyes
can not believe
we script the fiction
and see it flashed fulfilled
unable to detail
what is meaning
what is truth
these are our pasts reprising
haunted like an absence
taken from the real
like a vision
spun out of our control
they shall know this
and yet not know
run skipping through these ways
they touch no center
they are disjointed
and can not grasp these wholes
not like those anthems
more purposefully entailed
we peer across the lines to see
what might have been
sketching loosely
the patterns these would take
if set in motion
and founded in our world
this is not our way
it blocks and turns to dark
now comes the session
the moment of the change
we snap its outlines
and etch upon the mind
seeking the incursion
of yet another plane
one of lightness
with palatable ends
that we might savor
the die is cast, the stage is set
all alignments come to bear
if this be falling
what bottom shall we break?

ABOUT THIS COLLECTION[*]

This book is the first new issue from Eschaton Productions, Inc., which has been a long time in formation. Devoted to intellectual journeys through the darkness of the age, Eschaton will be releasing books in many fields, not only poetry. Collections like this one, however, will be the cornerstone for Eschaton Books.

The poems collected here follow a similar pattern to my most recent independently produced book, "Movement Through Depth", in that they represent the best 10% or so of my output over a two-year period, in this case from 1990 and 1991. Presented in chronological order, with one exception, they trace the course of my writing during these years.

As living unfolds, it appears to follow vectors on more complex planes. Our multi-dimensional existence traces patterns which we can only dimly sense, and which seed frustration in our urgent attempts to read the resulting runes. Cataclysmic change occurs to us, and is barely registered, yet subtle eddies in the currents of our time drive us to distraction. We live in the stone-walled prison that we have helped to build, yet our insistent spirit forever bids us to be free. It is an ugly place between, a zone of decay, a context always sinking "Beneath This Weight of Chain".

B.M.T.

---

* From the original 1993 "chapbook" edition.